THERE ARE TWO BIRDS AT MY WINDOW

Poems

ALLAN KOLSKI HORWITZ

DYE
HARD
PRESS

First published in 2012 by
Dye Hard Press
PO Box 783211
Sandton
2146
South Africa
http://dyehard-press.blogspot.com

ISBN 978-0-9870178-5-7

Many of these poems were previously published in Baobab,
Big Bridge, Botsotso, EAR, Golden Arrow,
Illuminations, ITCH, Letter to South Africa, New Coin,
New Contrast, Southern Rain, Ons Klyntji and Timbila

Cover, layout and illustrations – James de Villiers

CONTENTS

MZANSI, MY BEGINNING - MZANSI, MY END

26 October 2010   *After Allen Ginsberg's 'America'*

Mother and whore   father and rapist
for sure you a hard one to crack
no longer pariah   no longer reviled
you strut the world stage
veldskoen jackboots left behind
smug on the un-security council
toyi toyi turned into hilton ballroom glamour
your 'living wage for all' sweat-stained t-shirt now moth food
afro chic and sequins fill conference centres
as your 'better life' bitters in the hands
of global finance mafias and their local lackeys
      still no liberation from bantu education
      still no liberation from umlungu manipulation
you make me babbelas with your mandela mania
your fifa frolics   your renaissance that revives the begging bowl
your airconned malls sparkling with black diamonds and platinum
billionaires
you make me shriek at your taxis crammed with worker bees
sting disarmed as brakes fail and they roll
downhill into the deadend of cosatu/sacp posturing
      still savouring the honey of cabinet posts
      still threatening to end the alliance

but hey mzansi
you make me jump at your october jacaranda jozi streets
your boland spring magnificence   your south coast splash
you're the cradle of humanity where time walks on two feet
grips a bone between fingers and thumb
scoffs bunny chows and tamatie breedie
till you give me heartburn with the rest

of your daily dose of corruption scandal
        so it goes
        and just when i'm ready to come to blows
        turn my back on you and split
you make me jive with the cool kwaito style
of pantsula boys lounging at street corners
floppy hats hiding dagga drawn eyes
you make me oogle your model c goddesses
crowding wits and uct in dark shades and euro model bodies
rasta dread men quoting biko
as they parade in loxion and billabong
        ag what do they know?

your slap chips and coke meals long drowned
in sushi and cape wine
your cocktail sausages block the air vents of birthing whales
meandering across false bay as german tourists bathe in the spume
before driving back to the waterfront to buy zebra-skin briefcases
your deaths in boer detention long forgotten
as kwerekwere from congo nigeria and zim
clog your jails and cross and recross your borders
        i love you azania
        your generosity   your pyramid schemes
        your muti murders   your circumcision deaths
        your denial of sex plague   your free condomising
        your mercenaries   your peacekeepers
        your benoni hollywood meisie   your bollywood cricket spectacles
        your security fetish   your cash-in-transit heists
        your schools without playing fields   your white elephant stadiums
        your transgendered athletes   your steroid itchy rugger buggers

man   you got a nerve to hold endless workshops
trumpet endless promises
        as your shacktowns electrify but get flooded in winter

as your townhouses multiply in laughable tuscan affectation
as your kebbles build monstrous share castles that collapse
as your shaiks mock the intelligence of militants
but still i stroll along your promenades
and gape at the arching of your beaches
i climb your drakensberg and ache at your granite perfection
i leap over your gemsbok and straddle your giraffe necks
i drink castle and umqombothi at your weddings and funerals
praise the ancestors on all sides of the oceans

ja mzansi   you blow me away
so much to do   how did you find the time
to write a screenplay of tata ma chance delusions
idols and big brother scenarios
3rd rate american situations and isidingos
then make me cry and laugh with your succession shenanigans
your load-shedding and your arms dealing

but now out of the smoky streets of service delivery riots
comes your hour of truth   and i got to give it to you
when you seem down   all buggered and bloody
you find the strength to grab and make history
tell her "nooit, i ain't out for the count"
and write a new page for yourself and the planet
yo   what a mix masala   what a grend vibe
jirrah you're kwaai mzansi
don't make me skaam
you know i love you too much
kiss and don't talk
but you blast that vuvuzela one more time in my ear
and i'll moer you

12 MAY: MEMORIAM

I choose Mahler
the music is soft and sad
swelling always to crescendos:
twentieth century
romance and massacre

I light the candle

the music is inconclusive
on the edge of modern knowledge
we drift
making things
for money

the music
is
between the animal
and the machine
the human and the machine

proof of love is in
memory and
defiance of the death of
Spirit

whirling circles of gulls
grey clouds
covering you with the peace
you were crying for

I light the candle

IMPROVISATION IN SOPER ST

The drunken woman crashes against his car
  claws his door
    take me home I'll pay you   take me home . . .
he stares at her open mouth
  her bloodshot eyes
    take me home I can't die here I'll pay you
she wrenches the door open
  slumps in the seat
    number 5 soper st   I'll pay you
you can't leave me to die

   no   he can't leave her to die here
drunken old woman in the street on new year's eve
can't let her die on new year's eve
    the thugs will strip her
    the motherless will rape her
he can't leave her in the street

       new
         year to be
        of plenty:

no floods or erupting volcanoes
         only truth-telling repentant power-mongers
no bright-eyed children dying in car accidents
         only virgin births of compassionate buddhas
year in which no one will suffer heartache
            or backache or stomach ache
year in which everyone's team will win the cup
              win the jackpot
          wear the most stylish of clothes

year in which everyone will compose a hit song
   paint a masterpiece
year in which everyone will become famous
   have articles written about them

no! he can't leave the old woman
 in the bottled streets of new year's eve
 in the glass strewn streets
  in the firecracker boom-boom streets
 hundred song streets full of kids going too high

he drives her
 but the cops have sealed off berea
    got to stop crazies throwing fridges
    from the high rises
 now how the hell can he reach soper st?!

the cops tell him to take a one way wrong way
  and hope for the best
he takes the one way wrong way
   breaks thru the cordon
robots are red but he drives
   this way and that
finds soper in the warren of flats

at last! number 5
 the old woman blesses him
calls the caretaker to meet the brother who's saved her
calls the caretaker to witness the brother who hasn't asked for no money
 saved her life on new year's eve for no money!
  braved kidsrocketsbottlessmokebombsraging music
    and uncaring cops

the man opens her door

she tumbles out
the caretaker catches her before her old head
strikes the tar

  the man drives off

down soper st   a nineteen year old hooker with watermelon breasts
shrieks
    stop   I need you

  he drives on thru thebottlesthesmokethegyratingkids

                    *

The man gets home
prepares a cup of coffee
sits down and puts on ornette coleman

  cool

    then the two of them
  in unlikely but perfectharmony
      drive back   into berea

ANCIENT SECRETS OF TURMOIL

Earth was sundered here
  rock shorn to sheer face
then after the fire and ice
soil stepped up to carpet
and brown cloth filled the cracks
seeds landed borne by wind and water
  green mass vegetating food
        for red blooded creatures

now we come to this place
name it holy
    say it redeems
    the cramped minds of the human colony
and all this makes me wonder
for human art
    follows the forms
      of cosmic creation

  i am silent
hearing the stream song

        the stream has no peer

  the stream is too loud and too subtle
        too insistent when it runs
        for all other music

i listen to the stream massage
my hoarse anguished voice

FLIGHT: LARNACA - JOHANNESBURG

Dawn lays an egg
to fertilize Immensity

the harlot of Africa spreads rouge
on her leopard-skin

crossing their burning temples
pious Jews bind phylacteries

an acrobat sleeping on his wire
roasts over the boiling ocean

WHAT YOU DO FOR ME

Another day
        of frantic visions
   how mortal is our strut

dragging feet
on too tired legs
altogether leaden
hopes dash about
hardly daring to breathe
as the hours mock us
     mock our games
  make us fill each chamber
      before putting the gun
        to the head

another day when your love
has to bring not just a stay
of execution
but a full reprieve

and as I walk away
from the scaffold   the firing squad
the wired chair   the lethal syringe
    it is your presence
  your hand more real than my own
      that walks beside me
that appoints the road
        to peace

WHITE HORSES FLECKING INGRID
Three Anchor Bay (19 February 2008)

The child is the dark shadow of the
soldiers on guard with their rifles,
saracens and batons
the child is present at all assemblies
and law-giving
the child peers through the windows of
houses and into the hearts of mothers
this child who wanted only to play in
the sun at Nyanga is everywhere
the child grown to the man treks on
through all Africa
the child grown into a giant journeys
over the whole world without a pass

Ingrid Jonker

White horses
green water
rubbish shivers in the wind
blouberg squat
undifferentiated blocks across the bay
rusted anchor
still holding ground against the surf
   against the tide

year after year:
   you could not stand against the tide
   you were sucked in
   you threw yourself in
   you screamed
   you laughed
   you bubbled
   you were silent

once you entered the waves your father
   shouted in his sleep
but he never spoke
never betrayed the words he slept with under his pillow
      between his legs
   so mean and nasty and twisted
 who could credit he was guardian of the nation's dreams?
      begetter of your lonely breasts

      Ingrid
you walked into the sea
you did not walk back

here
in the shadow of the mountain
between the island and the bay
         you opened your mouth
         your heart flooded for good

   how many more lost children have drowned?

                    *

Broken black rocks raging
yet mute like your tears
seagulls cracking whips
wind whip
vicious and clean
forlorn city
wasted hour
cruise ship blues
enjoy the miracle of southeasterly clouds!

          i am drunk
wasted after toasting the chief of police on trial
   his jamming the wheels of justice
toasting the fermenting   the ferreting out of secrets
   underlying arms deals
 toasting the causes for power shutdowns

    drunk toasting
the Zim dictator
  his sons and daughters come down in their droves
     they're starving

drunk on the piss of the rabid white albatross trashing Africa
   drunk on the boiling jackboots it brings down
 on the heads of blackbirds

all in Ingrid
 i'm all in

 all in all
i toast you too
    here

your face on the book

                    *

Don't return from down there
salt water sweeter than tears
settle for seaweed
  settle for iodised eyelashes
stay comfy on a hollow sandbank

accept you were born in a bad time

callous imbecility

accept drowning's
a wise solution to the clamour
of uncouth arty men
            tasting your juice and finding it tasty
        wanting to suck   and suck   and suck . . .

accept   death made you famous
and we quote you in parliament

accept   this barbed drunken country
of famished scorpions

 accept   we like our poets dead
so we can study them at leisure
and make cuts
            make cults
package their poems in red tape for schools
make mince meat of them for babbelas braais
drown them in entitlement's gravy

drown them!   drown them!

                    *

Drown you?

COMRADES IN ARMS

Comrade A who boats on the blue lagoon
comrade B who hunts along the promenade
comrade C who scrapes the dust from a philosopher's brow
comrade D who strokes the breasts of a temptress
comrade E who hitches himself to an unbroken stallion
comrade F who runs away from his shadow

all these comrades ponder:
   the taunting of time
   the paradox of progress
   the conundrum of a grand climax

all these comrades get together in the evening
to chew fat
  share confidences of the heart and loins

all of them including

comrade U who feeds the lions in his bedroom
comrade V who offers himself to fat virgins
comrade W who surfs a tectonic plate
comrade X who sings in harmony with a raging typhoon
comrade Y who picks his sores
comrade Z who enters a parallel dimension

  they want to come to rest
but only after some infamous act of damnation
  some spectacular act of salvation

IF

If I take a vow   and   break   it

If I take a vow   and bend   it

If I take a vow   and   beat   it

      bewilder it
       bewitch it
    berate it
     bemoan it
        befuddle it

Have I taken a vow?

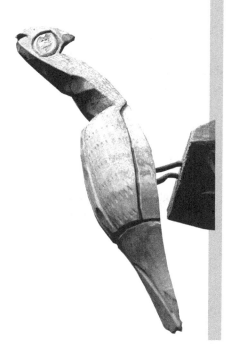

PIVOTAL DREAM

The iron roof makes music

midnight rain glides in
to drown lawns
       prepare them for sunshine

books sprawl across my eyes
leftovers ignite my appetite

no doubt about it
       been a good day

    saw no mangled bodies
       was not clawed by raw talons
    had to pity no beggar
      was not outraged by a headline
ducked away from no shoot-out in a shopping mall
     heard no crying children
       tasted no dumb defeat
     touched no crass nerve

engaged with others thru the medium of smiles

and tonight I will sleep deeply
      record a pivotal dream

OCEAN MOTHER

      Just
the hush
  hum of her great sprawling body
shifting   drifting along her hard bed
  sucking her breath on the shore
letting her wavy breasts curl and break
  wash gladly
        against the brown ribbon of earth

  to just sit at sunset
by the ocean

UNDER THE SUMMER BLUE SKY OF TROYEVILLE

Under the summer blue sky of Troyeville
Next to a marimba disguised as a bench
You spun out your threads
Hands arching in the air
Voice jumping from detail to detail
You described old women and old clothes
The grandmother you adore
Who had struggled for the people
Now enjoyed soap opera
Political flame doused as the wheelchair makes pliant
Then you spoke of your breakdown
In the corporate desert
The need to find a reason to work

Under the summer blue sky of Troyeville
You smoked cigarette after cigarette and drank beer
And your face moved and your voice moved
Sending messages of which I am not sure
Your arms and neck turning from side to side
And I imagined kissing your back
Wondering if once again I would
Fall in love
With a delicate woman

WHEN I READ YOUR WORDS

When I read your words
I read mine
When I read your words
I read between the lines
When I make words
I read yours
When I make words
I let the stream flow
When I read your words
I feel my stream flow
When I fix my words
I fix yours
When I fix yours
I make mine sharper
When I read between your lines
I read between mine
Then I join our lines
To bind the book of our times

SURVIVAL OF THE STARS

On the edge of the valley
a muezzin calls to the setting sun
  dozing sunday
slow streams of cars

the muezzin sings languid sad songs
  urges his god to anoint us
    us to anoint him

the muezzin implores all believers and unbelievers
in dusty desert villages   in caravan towns
  in spiraling cities and dense sewerless suburbs
calls all those sprawled by fountains of imperial majesty
    on sultanic divans near scented gardens
  calls phantoms bearing scimitars and veils
  along busy throngs past market stalls

the muezzin calls piety and respect
into the world of work and profit-taking
as a man and his dogs walk the kopje
pushing forward in the fading light
  breathing   no panting!   with the joy of space
of sky and sound carried along the valley and its slopes

                              *

the man and his dogs
reach the squat khaki marker
erected by a pious empire in memory of fallen lackeys
                    colonial servants of war
                    brought across the ocean

to fight and die
for another's glory
another's wealth

called by the empire upon which the sun never set
called to render service
then once disease or artillery or horses hooves
trampled the life out of them
this empire commissioned their memorial pile
recorded their sacrifice
their duty filled per and beyond
expectation

from across the ocean they came
with horses and tents and beds
to serve the white folk:
their masters: administrators   merchants   missionaries

now the man and his dogs circle the memorial:

TO THE MEMORY OF BRITISH OFFICERS
NATIVE
NCO'S AND MEN
VETERINARY ASSISTANTS
NALBANDS
AND
FOLLOWERS OF THE INDIAN ARMY
WHO DIED IN SOUTH AFRICA
1899 -1902

Musalman
Christian
Zorbustrian
Hindu
Sikh

coloured servants and soldiers   come to the call of the bugle
        come to south africa to serve the white devil:
            golden veins running along his arms

        (no doubt rhode's dragged the stones for the marker
        himself
        along the ridges and the rande
        of the farm that became the observatory
        under which the white veins ran into billions)

                        *

man and his dogs
smoke column in the east above the last mine dumps
golden hills of jozi sunset
skyscraper colouration ebbs majestic
reflects
wraps up the ridge with its peaceful towers
silver globes' exploration of the stars
silent rock gardens with aloe stalks
foreign and native plants greening the ridge flanks
deep space hum in which the blip of guns
or dogs or muezzins
  fades
            is irrelevant
    is impossible to trace

                        *

all falls into the time stream
  all falls off the slopes

of this kopje
this high holy place
for zionist preachers and their congregants
white robes   white doeks   staffs   plastic bottles
  of Holy Water

  they bring chickens to sacrifice
    severed sheep heads
they bring their woes and hallelujahs
all calling the ancestors
to bring rain   and money   and love

                          *

zionists light candles in crevices
leave them smoking in rock alcoves
pray for wind to lift flames and purge the hillside
          purge demons from the body of the earth
          from the stinking body of the sinner
from the drinker   the dicer   the conman of disease and death
  the wild merchant who peddles children
    cons beggars into parting with their blind eyes
    cons street corners into sheltering whores

so fire blackens the slopes
savages green shoots of spring
swats the shrubs and stunted trees

and on that scorched earth
the man and his dogs find paper crosses
inscribed with the names
                          of the dead

dead by diarrhea
dead by coughing
dead by sweating

names and dates

names and dates
of the dead

anointed with semen
bathed in vaginal fluid
a plague rewarded their highpoints
with a climb
to heaven but first taste
hell
            the virus said
first taste hell
have hell rammed up and come out of your arse
  clog your teeth
   scale your skin
   grey you
            grey you

   first taste hell

                    *

the zionists come to the hillside to save
the thin ones
and the thinner ones
   the guts   aching stream of water
the heavy-breathing ones
            the ones with mottled peeling skin

the ones almost too weak to climb the kopje

they bring their water to wash off the semen
   the vaginal juice
they bring plastic coke bottles filled
with potent flowing fluid

they spread their arms to the sky
  they call out
and the congregants face down
swim in the voice of the chosen one
   the one who will take their pain and raise it high
for the Maker to make light
            to carry off and bear away

                    *

the man and his dogs pass the zionists
and he requests they preserve the green slopes
   the winding paths
and the zionists   their white crisp robes red
with the sand of the kopje
smile   and the man smiles in return
and he vows   to bring bags to carry off the bottles
            and the chicken heads and the sheep heads
            and the robes left dangling on the branches
            the stumps of burnt bushes

he vows with them to keep
the holy presence
but he knows he speaks
of another holiness
            theirs is too close to their flesh

to the other world of the already dead

he knows they do not see *his* holy mountain
  do not feel *his* elation as the sun sets
and the horizon lifts and the cityscape
unfolds and the dogs race madly up and down the slopes
    sniffing and barking and being free

          *

the man walks on the ridge every sunday
he greets the zionists and the vagabonds
who come to wash
and he observes the plastic and the ripped cloths multiply
the fires come quicker and quicker
to burn and blacken
      and he prays for the kopje
      prays for the holy space
      prays for the zionists and the thin people
    the frightened people   the suffering people

he prays and the blessed light
survives as dusk shelters his eyes

the beauty of the kopje must always survive

  always   survive!

  in order for those who need its beauty to
survive

for beauty enables
the holy to survive

beauty enables . . .

　　　so　survive!

　　　　　*

the man and his dogs
walk the kopje as sunset shines and rusts the sky
the valley below
echoes with the muezzin

they walk at ease
uplifted by the high place
walk into the steady evening
with their hearts light

lighter than any history

they walk knowing that nothing counts beyond
　　　　this hour

soft poetry of the kopje
sad　　but not mournful
footsteps on the path
 paws pattering the dust

　　　　joburg at rest

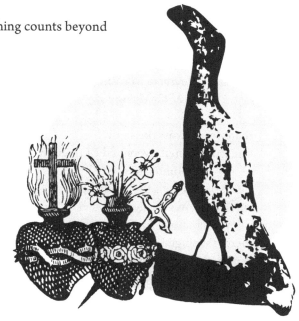

BIRD'S EYE: KAROO FLIGHT

Light lines across the reddish
 brown
roads break thru   velddust
  emptiness

    so much space after the cramp

        too many calls in the street
      too many pushing outside the queue
            too many queues
       fever as the halfbaked loaf collapses
       and curses the baker
        the gingerbreadman
         the schoolboy   the mother

           i am sick
        of the strutting selfish
       oaf who blocks his neighbour
        the nurse who falls asleep
        over the dying baby

roads lead across the sand
transcontinental rivers of dust riven by
        antediluvian waters
sweat passes onto the sandy bed
cloud shadows the floor
  i'm in a bubble   knifethin stratosphere
merciless singer moaning blues
causing havoc in the jetstream
these silver machines   these elegant baubles
  i want to handle them   i want to fly!

i want more control over the trivial
mindclamps must not drag me down
pettifogging

far below
        far   far below
the valleys stretch flatnosed
  meteorite craters   gaunt declensions
musty coves of devastation

                    *

light lines across the reddish
brown
        roads break thru   velddust

  emptiness
so much space after the cramp

    flying over the karoo i admire scars
        of battle   tectonic ocean battle

    billion plankton burialground
rough sandy waste   rough   grinding
                grandeur

PHOTOGRAPHING HIPPOS

Under the flame tree on the estuary bank
late light vibrating with the ripple of waters
    she stands   all charm and power
pink skirt clinging to the bell of her legs
  fabric wafting with soft ocean wind

holding a camera   fixing perspective
      she levels her eyes
makes the sound and the sign of OM
 and I watch her lean forward as pink billows
    she herself an object to study

beyond   in the channel
hippos push up   gigantic heads
  gums protrude   pink runnels of flesh
     yawn and gape
   as sunset stretches strong color

hippos have all the time they need
  to feel breeze shiver their wet flanks
while under the flame tree the undulating woman
      adjusts the camera
 makes the sound and the sign of OM

  light drains   skirt swallows her legs
     hair spreads wings
I watch her under the flame tree
   as hippos submerge
 and she snaps shades of blubbering sunset

D.

mirage in my desert

how untruthful to name you delusion
winter sun on my body
i stretch to embrace

alone in this unknown country
inflamed with you
far away as a star

you are more than a mirage in my desert

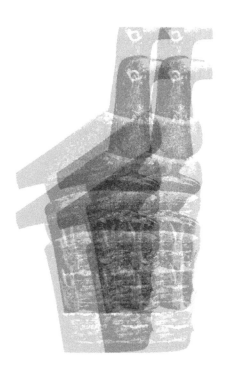

THE NIGHT I FINISHED THE PLAY ABOUT BRETT KEBBLE

I went to the spot where the tycoon was executed
Stood in front of the small iron cross attached to the bridge rails
Overlooking the highway
And took a photo of the cross and the bridge and the two flower pots
His secretary had placed there
And wondered what went thru his mind just before
The appointed killer pumped seven bullets
Into him
Then I remembered the R80 million in insurance he'd placed
Just weeks before his death
After he'd been kicked off the boards of the four main companies
He'd controlled and swindled for years
       Yes, he knew the game was over and couldn't face
       The prison wall staring him in the face
       Besides he loved his kids and wanted to provide for them
       In death
       While he couldn't do so alive

I stood there
Almost one in the morning
Early spring
Chill in the air
And saw him slumped in his big Merc
Engine idling
Blood draining out of him

I stood there watching the cars pass on the highway
And then I tried to step back
For history to arrive and finish the job

CRUMBS AT KEI MOUTH

At the start of each day
the men and women of the township over the hill
rise from the pink and lavender matchbox houses
they have been allowed to inhabit
        and trudge to and from the sites
        that bring them bread:
    the caravan park   the holiday flats
        the hotels   the restaurants

brown with lumpy bodies
mouths missing teeth   feet missing shoes
  broad noses shining with sweat
these men and women of the township
trudge to and from the seaside resort
getting blacker and blacker against the white skins
     of the hotel owners   the restaurant owners
     the petrol station owner   the estate agent
     the librarian   the fishing tackle shop assistant
     the tourists   the travelers swallowing
            the whole road with their mega-tires

each day they arrive at and depart
and each day they say to themselves
  "if only destiny can be rewritten"

each day looking for the crumbs
    sprinkled round the town at the mouth
    of the historical river

EASTER

Dagga afternoon in Natal Street
the beer mama at Celeste Mansions doing fine
Easter Monday and the resurrection
of the opposition to the ANC looks doubtful
after the election on Wednesday:
years of GEAR moving sideways
    backwards?

after lunch everyone crawls into bed
dreams of cheap prices at the spaza
strokes sensitive spots till
doorbells ring in the after-life and
Jehovah's Witnesses
reset the boundaries of debate

remember Hani?
Hani?
Chris Hani
the communist   the MK leader

it's easter again
we went to vote for the third time since Codesa bore its fruit
    but it was yr blood, Chris
      finally carried us over the cataract
            to elections

exile   so many stories
  Quatro and others
underground days when fear
of infiltration made men paranoid
when Soviet corruption

made liberation
posture the Freedom Charter

but watching the long lines at the Yeoville recreation centre
I was reminded of
the dead days
the greed and brutality:
      Sea Point
      Dutchmen throwing bergies
      into the bowels of their cop vans

recalled
the mournful drone of the foghorn
Rivonia locked up on Robben Island
bruin sweepers keeping the Slegs-Blanks clean
hopeless pass offenders crammed into Caledon Square
the Parade's stalls mournful at night
doek-headed Pondo women   felt-hatted men
maids and gardeners queueing
for busses and trains to the 'nowhere' that was Nyanga
  then back in the morning to the 'somewheres'
that were Claremont and Camps Bay

      better times:
  ocean and snoek
yellow foam at Sandy Bay covering pale breasts
white wine sprayed across the lips
of our Cape of Good Hope and sun worshippers

  then
      Hani at the picket
KFC owned by Jomo Sono in Twist Street
      centralized bargaining
you came to wear the strikers' t-shirt

you stood with the picket and you did not make a speech
        you made a stand

now the unions support crooks   pervert mandates
the new police force roadblocks onto kwerekwere
wabenzi cram share options into their bras
send directors over the company moon
'big five' malls strut as game farms stock up for dollars
aids ghosts wither at funerals
get drunk on a cocktail of african potato and vitamins
councillors slow track RDP shacks for kickbacks
and   as always   the greyhaired boyish bankers
caricature the insane

yes, that's some of what we've got to deal with
left over leaves browning in the unkempt streets

but today
I remember you Chris Hani
your quiet dignity

wonder where we'd be now without your being
martyred
        yr spirit is still here
years of bitter-sweet freedom
   and   it is better

but how much better
would it have been with your
   leadership

Remember you well   Chris Hani

SUMMER NIGHT IN YEOVILLE

The women are out
Streets slide with their sway
Walking in pairs
Skin-tight slax
Breast-hugging tops
How can men not stare?

The women are out
Elegant clicking heels
Sure-footed and free
Strolling to dance
Rolling hips and buttocks
How can men not smile?

The women are out
Night perfume
Breathes deep
Pregnant with wild seed
They fill the starry universe
With throbbing assent

How can men remain in
When women are out?

EGO IN GAZA

She whom I need
betrays me by disappearing
as I clutch at her cleavage
does not answer when I call
blows my kiss away and laughs
because she has seen me
with the wantons at the corner
of Obscurity and Fame

she spits on my need
derides my late night tossing
scorns my needle
rips at my tongue as it curls for the
white powder of Recognition

she whom I need has no need
to declaim fragments of profane scripture
paint figments with the misty breath of Illusion

she laughs at my (unfathomable)
need to applaud myself

                    *

pathetic flab
beneath the tough sounding metres

laurel leaf slipped over his eyes
sprig stuck in his throat

rapture of the spirit
prisoned

*

bad patch
even cabbage won't grow
nightmares of abandonment
raise weeds
raise hell with the gardeners

where are days of Faith of Beauty
when radiant steps hold up the sun

why should this life turn us
to drink deadly waters
eat the snakes of Betrayal
sleep holding Whoredom

where are the days of Faith   of Beauty
days when a ready eye greets the sun

*

my child   he glows still
I catch his warmth and press it to my lips

I so much fear him
drowning in lakes of Greed and Uncouthness

I want to listen to him play in Glory

WINTER DAY IN BARBERTON
(*Naming the Supergroup*)

Submarine volcanics

primitive lavas
 'komatites'
34,000 million years old

invasive granites
up to 15km thick

encased   with
                    irongoldmanganesenickelantimony
copperbismuthigolidemercuryarsenicchrysotile
        barytessilverkaolinverdirtequartz
    porphyrygraphitemagnesite

                    *

past blackened winter veld
dried fields of rasping mielie stalks
imagined but unsustainable hope
boosting the solace he needs to fill the place
of perished dreams
        he looks up at the goldrush skies
    bleak with salty gray clouds
                    then around at the town
        and chants:

the veldskoen shop doesn't make veldskoene
only repairs what's falling apart

the vetkoek den's pancakes drown in syrup
so saccharine the lemon tastes sweet
the curio co-op is drab with empty colours
three legged pots limp on two little stubs
the painted chef on the butchery window smiles at
his red sausages and decomposing primate fingers
the phoenix hotel motionless under renovation
waits for its cooks now camped in the mountains
the only sign of grace is a boy whistling down main street
tearing open a packet of chips

he chants to himself: all this clowning on top of
the 15km thick granite slabs anchoring Barberton

MY SECRET LOVE

You are a secret
I do not parade you
I keep you for night

Dark jewel glowing
Warm and soft and firm
I clasp you
Twinning arms and lips and legs
I hold you
Opalescent

And while the sun shines
Incandescent life maker
I dream of the depths
And bow
To another source of
Intense heat and tenderness

I dream of the night
When I clasp you
Velvet lovely glowing

SUPERMODEL

She wears a pout as long as her legs
Raises her voice till it grates
Closes her mind to all thoughts not of herself
Opens her ears only to the echo of her whine

She wears dresses to titillate her figure
Uses paint to show off her blush
She is shallow as a puddle of milk
On the catwalk

EVA HAROUN BLOGS FROM TAHRIR SQUARE

The dictator warns the people: I am stubborn
The people respond: each of us has 3 PhDs in stubbornness

The dictator warns: I will crush you like a dung beetle rolls shit
The people respond: we are the grass that gives life to the cow

The dictator warns: I will descend like a hawk from the sky, tear you
                            limb by limb
The people respond: we are all field mice armed with the power of flight

The dictator warns: I will blot you out like an eclipse of the sun
The people respond: we will shine like the moon with her full belly

The dictator warns: I will unleash your sons, my soldiers, to beat you
The people respond: we will offer them the bread and meat you scoff at
                            your banquets

The dictator warns: I will call in my paymasters from across the ocean
The people respond: we will show them the tombs of our ancestors

The dictator warns: I will divert the waters of the sacred river
The people respond: we with our sweat will flood the parched plains

The dictator warns the people: I will seduce you with my myth and my
                            tanks
The people respond: we will become heroes in our own story

                            *

The people gather in the square.
The people in their hundreds of thousands.

And the people dance. Raise placards.
The people offer flowers to the soldiers.
Offer flowers to each other.
The people wait.

The dictator summons his generals.
Schemes with his cronies till dawn.
The dictator calls for clandestine action.
The people sing songs and rally each other.
Though his cudgels break their bones.
Though the walls of their houses collapse.
Though flour runs out in the bakeries.

The people sit. They sit in the square
The dictator offers a new cabinet.
An election. Offers an end to emergency rule.
But how many times has he lied?
How many times before promised change?

The people sit and the dictator puffs up his chest:
Once I am gone another strong man will replace me.
Another strong man.
You will see.
You are a rabble that needs to be led.

The people hold high their placards in the square.
There is no choice but to believe.
The people must believe
They do not need another bully.
Another cabal.

The people sit. Day after day, they sit.
And this sitting shakes the dictator's henchmen.
Frightens foreign powers who back him.

They sound the alarm.
Threaten chaos if he leaves.
But the people chant in the square.
Chant by the roadside.
Resist the thugs and the warnings
Till the dictator does a deal
And the armed forces replace him.

The people celebrate with song and dance.
Celebrate with poems and speeches.
Then the people disperse and return to their old lives.
Their jobs and their families.
Their weddings and funerals.

Who will now keep the flame burning?
Who will set fear aside?
Draft a just constitution. Hold fair elections.
Revise the policies that make life so hard.
Who will ensure that the generals keep their word?

The flame must be fed by the guardians.
Those who will not retreat.
Those in whom the flame burns brightest.
The flame must burn strong
Along the valley of the great river.
In the marshes and desert.
The people must hoist up the standard.
Push away the old tiredness.
The yoke of yore.
.
The people shoulder the question mark that hangs over them.
They take up the chant.
The people rally round the guardians.
The people become stronger than the strong man.

The people become their own heroes.

This has been Eva Haroun from Tahrir Square.
May I be a mother of this revolution!
The mother of a new time!
I, the first woman singing to you
Of the uprising.

NERUDA'S POETIC HOUSES

Nefteli Ricardo Reyes y Basoalto
bought and decorated three houses:
    la Isla Negra   two hours west of Santiago on the Pacific coast
    la Sebastiana in Valparaiso   overlooking the harbour
    la Chascona   lighting the backstreets of Bellavista

'I built my house(s) like a toy house and I play in it from morning till night'

and play you did though aching
the wound in your soul engraved
more deeply than the tattoos on a celebrity
      those who require at least 5 min of tv exposure per day
      visiting a war-torn area to comfort refugees
        adopting a poor child from the slums or an African village
          launching a perfume
          launching a salad dressing
          launching a range of t-shirts

you lived long and saw much
became perhaps an old man smelling of urine
      herpes flaring every second week
      yet still a romantic worshipper of birth and rebirth
          an ever swelling ocean of feeling
you who travelled and collected
brought back to Chile treasures of an astute eye
because she had given you so many

the lives of workers real for you
the struggles of the poor to not stay poor
years of faith despite exile and defeat

you could not just stand under that bitter blinding sun
you needed to dream
needed the draw of waves
an immense view of the ocean
your eye and nose alert to the nuance and fist of excess
celebrated the jungle of Temuco's Eden
the testimonies of rivers and mountains

now I read you again after many years
and the grinding plantations of the United Fruit Company
come back to memory
      those more ancient peoples of the Americas
      trapped under the net of Europe
   by the horse   the cross   the rabid disease

I drink the juice you squeezed out of that history
and your wounds:

> *"My poems took being, in travail*
> *retrieved from the thorn, like a penance,*
> *wrenched by a seizure of hands, out of solitude;*
> *or they parted for burial*
> *their secretest flower in immodesty's garden.*
> *Estranged to myself, like shadow on water,*
> *that moves through a corridor's fathoms,*
> *I sped through the exile of each man's existence . . ."*

intoxicated by the plasma in your breast
at night in its panther dark
you made journeys to corners of the globe
points of the zodiac
and there encountered
      "death opening roadways and doorways"

Pablo   diplomat senator
who would not live *"like a root in a shadow"*
your green ink fertile and sprouting
sometimes grandiloquent sometimes too rich
          but you still stir
keep me awake reading and sounding
your sinuous throaty Spanish
your ripe compassion
recognition of every *"man with a withering rose*
in his hand, dustily fallen to dust"

and who was that man
if not yourself

          all poets

SEASONING

The season is ready
Purple flowers
Cascade in the streets
Now red flowers come to join them
All eager for the thunder showers
The crashes of electric storms
All eager for the summer
When a breeze comes
Opening then closing
Windows

Baring chests and scooping skirts
This season of gasping skies
I drive myself through the city
And I fear no evil

After the breeze
Cool and rejoicing
Comes the cyclic rain

DRUNKEN NEED

Phantom of starlit avenues
tongue-tying muse
curved statue of a goddess
sweet groined virgin who coaxes

    when was it i awoke from sleep
    to find you beside me?
    when did the song in my head
    became your voice?

your voice: a growl   a screech
            a sibilant sigh

then you disappear   delinquent
mock me for hearing   feeling you
inciting ghosts in the night
to throw stones against my window
let blood run down the glass
       so i drive out in distress
scour the streets
dare them to throw you up
till under a grand tree
in a suburb of respectable robbers
    i find you undressing

flushed   i advance
      yes you   phantom
wild with words to wreck my destiny
but as i reach out
you step back
      always a step ahead

always a glimpse away

gracious cocky phantom
i wrestle with loneliness
but i fear my fever
will settle for nothing less
than to die in your arms

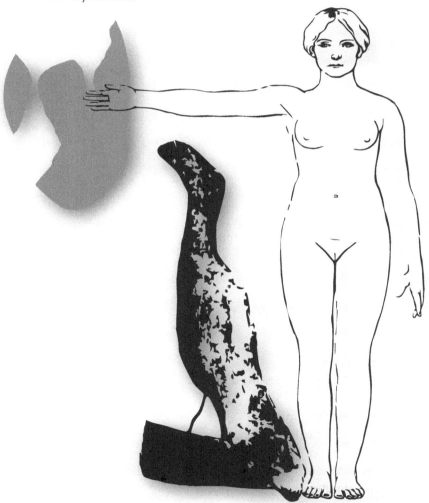

PORTRAIT OF JOSIAH MADSUNYA (1959)
Photograph by Bob Gosani

Bearded man in a suit
fist clenched   raised
your eyes fix the viewer

township dog at your side
eyes and fangs poised
    ready to defend   and attack
you both stand   ready
for the stray eye   all and any intent
of the stranger

shacks and buildings
other dogs
            shadows
Josiah Madsunya
        you tell us yours is the spirit
of no surrender
            to all the fates
            that privilege
    cause hardship

proud   ready to accept
the challenge of chance
            and sanctify the rising of the sun
proud man
            son of Africa
    its new and old cities
grasslands   plains   mountains
      son of Abantu
standing resolute

resolute for all time

and we salute you   Josiah Madsunya
affirm the spirit of 'no surrender'
even as we turn our eyes away
from your eyes

        too pure   too strong
   your look into our crumpled greed
        our jumbled intentions

   we salute what we should be

CENSUS

They came to the shelter for battered women
enumerators in orange t-shirts
        they came to fill forms
                to ask and record

and the battered women peered out
from behind their bruises   their blemishes
peered out with sour looks and grimaces
and touching their welts and their scars
        stumbled from their beds
                shuffled out of the tv room
    crawled out from the cracks

the battered women in the shelter
came out to give answers
                confirm the bare facts
so proud to be reckoned alive
among those whose needs
need to be written down
                researched   made allowance for

standing in front of the enumerators
it was almost like being famous
this being counted as if you counted

SONG OF THE EWE, THE SHEPHERD AND THE RAM

She lay in the bush
gored by a ram
    she lay bleeding

she hobbled back to the kraal
seeking comfort
    offered herself   (it was a time of pain)
yes she nuzzled me
  whispered words of devotion

out in the bush the ram paced

there in the kraal she nuzzled me
offered her wetness
    her warmth

the ram cracked rock
  split his hooves
but she pulled me in

  i shivered with joy

i shivered
knowing in the morning
    wounds healed
she would return to the ram in the bush

ANGOLAN STICKS

Heart-shaped bars on the window

night dunes shed their grains
wind crosses the river
to perfume the house
where I read Kapuschinski's account
of Angola in 1976:

sweltering Luanda

water runs out
rubbish smothers vultures
luxurious weapons
tooled and greased
in Pretoria Washington Moscow
stutter across the blast of landmines

night dunes sand lids
moths flap off their power
I sleep behind bars in East London
shielded from rotting armies
container cities where colonists crammed
degraded treasure onto sinking boats

wind curls the river
white birds stalk the beach
three pronged imprints marking
denying the tide
while amputees stick rancid flesh
through the window

raw stumps jamming iron hearts

58

HE DOES NOT KNOW HER/HE KNOWS HER

He does not know her
yet he did
        brief   abiding
        in halflight

only the curve of her cheek
slope of her breasts
curious ridge of her upper teeth
known

        all known fleetingly

      *

they hold each other
in the still room
overlooking the ocean
   waves in their veins
    rising up to drown out
    the swells on the beach

their hearts and this hotness

her soft voice
   'this is my first time'
he is silent
   'my first time'

she slips off her dress
pulls him towards her
        his silence dogged on her neck

                gruff with awe

    her voice
        'are you mine?'

    her voice naked
        his hands make her burn
                'are you mine?'
            'are you   mine?'

    she is naked   caressing him

        'yours forever
                            yours
            fo r   e ve   r

                    *

    his mad seed lined her
        dumb   explosion of silence
        after panting

            i am yours . . .

        then   years and   years

        that longing
                . . . to be so filled

ASSET MANAGER IN TRAFFIC

Managing
one billion

one billion rand   income for one million families

morning
i drive thru the city
       it covers the veld
  is highways gardens   shacks
      dense boiling human colony

core of this planet molten lava
all planets derived from primal gas

by the roadside
a woman suckles her baby
   i drive past her sweet mother's milk

      car after car

i am responsible for one billion: shares buildings bonds
      derivatives futures . . .

mother does not look up
cars passing worth millions of human hours

earth made up of different layers of matter
morning a shaken scatter of purple flowers
baby sucks the sweet milk
highways clog with cars worth trillions of rand euros dollars yen

and this earth morning stirs me
    the planet is humming
layer of soil just a few hundred meters
    core steams and froths

i look up   clouds drip one billion pieces of buys and sells
paper all paper all paper a ll pa p er al l p a p er
clogs the skies

the mother looks down
baby looks up
    but soaked in the car fumes
    the baby is blind

ABDULLAH'S TOP TO BOTTOM DOLLAR

Linder Auditorium, 19 November 2007

        Born under the mountain
       loosened by wind
      made playful by the minstrel band
        he is before his instrument
            the keys on which he plays
          the world

   Abdullah Ibrahim seats himself   brings palm to palm
        bows to us

three men on stage in black before brown wooden panels

        then he tunes the air
        speaks in the language before
         WORD
        taps his foot and sways:
          rich is his sheen
         warm and alive his fingers

three brown men in black before brown wooden panels

          goema
       he is goema and swirls of American
       anguish
       the steady beat
       of falls in the Amatola mountains

       a new music   a full music
       a new/old music in Cape Town   New York
       in so many cities between and beyond

three men on a brown wooden stage in black

ja Dollar　　nou ja　Dullah
the life of exile
sharp teeth of a snoek
you　also had to beg and borrow
you　also had to carry sorrow

but tonight you celebrate art of your motion in airy vibration
leave all else aside
and we drink in
rise to our feet in acclaim

we say ja
ja ja!
to mature　subtle　moving
music　made by
three brown men on stage in black before brown wooden panels

TAVERN GIRL

She was a tavern girl
 sloppy breasts
 forked tongue
 fatty thighs

at night
she would suck a peppermint
   paste on tight jeans

at night
 roll her eyes   and loll
by the barside
        suck hungry eyes
        sip out their glasses

later
      away from the noisy bottles
she would stagger into the alley
          stagger to pee
still later
          when the door was locked
she would crouch in the alley
for the owner's cock

                    *

in the morning she would still be thirsty
in the morning she hated her smelly pussy
in the morning she would try but never wash herself clean
in the morning she would sharpen a knife
but retreat from her scars

and in the evening she would be ready
again learn to love

                                 anyone

   for the price of a drink

           *

at night she would crouch in the alley to pee
at night she would be thirsty
       till the owner's son forced in his cock

           *

there is no one she cannot love

she squeezes into tight jeans
 sloppy breasts on the bar
thirsty
    fans her pussy

           *

closing time   sip the owner's brother
       in the morning   sharpen a knife
 in the evening   suck a peppermint

     thirsty   thirsty

      thirsty

SPRINGING, AT LAST

The hedge trembles
pushes out tips of baby tissue
       light and tender
   coiled   waiting
  whispering

'we are winter weary
  waste no more time
       each midnight whipping
the surface white   frost knuckling
       windscreens sheet over
   chilled and chafed'

in the new light i check branches
the oak fumbles
  empty sticks give olive
signals to prize open eyes
       and peek at the sky

i
spy and dance
the cold king is relenting and the queen's warm hand
covers his hand   making it soft
  the bitter bone of the low sun
rising now
sap struggles to surge
       but surge it does

     go green
     go green
      grows   green

I WANT YOU TO BE BEAUTIFIED

You will not accept my kiss
    you keep your lips tight
    teeth clenched to deny
you will not caress me
    except in the small hours
    while dreaming of another
you will not live with me
the outsider not from your clan
      you plan a house in your home town
      where everyone knows you

but I want to buy you a dress
adorn and deepen your skin
I want you to shine in this garment
    let my love
be reflected back by its beauty
    let my love spill
onto the fabric and shine
    you forever
          even when I am dead   for you
          even when your next lover
          threatens to slash and destroy
          my tribute   my joy
          my gift to your sculpture

I want to give you a dress
drape you in the adoring folds of my dejection

NAMING

A 4th grade   low ranking official   gets a cul-de-sac
a 3rd grade   low ranking official   gets an alley

a 2nd grade   middle ranking official   gets a lane
a 1st grade   middle ranking official   gets a side street

a 2nd grade   high ranking official   gets a main street
a 1st grade   high ranking official   gets an avenue

a 4th grade   senior high official   gets a boulevard
a 3rd grade   senior high official   gets a freeway

a 2nd grade   senior supervising high official   gets an airport
a 1st grade   senior supervising high official   gets a town

a 2nd grade   special senior supervising high official   gets a city
a 1st grade   special senior supervising high official   gets a region

a zero grade dictator gets a country

REFUGEES
(For Ghassan Khanafani)

Trucks are loaded
  beds fridges linen toys
      the past and the future
trucks loaded at speed
    at gunpoint

trucks are loaded
  children dogs birds mice
    the past and the future
loaded by the innocent   and the weak
      loaded by the enemy
          loaded by collaborators

trucks are loaded
  paintings silverware books dice
      the past and the future
trucks loaded
        maps opened
  borders evaded   borders crossed
borders spat and trampled on
          then blessed

trucks are loaded
  photos letters diaries wills
      the past and the future
loaded trucks become a convoy of
stalled generations tripping in minefields
hanging on barbed wire

trucks loaded with memory

frag the imagination of children
make them cry

*

trucks loaded at homes   then driven to
camps

trucks dump in camps
camps to take the place of
places of work   places of worship
places of study   places of healing

camps to
hold people in check
in reserve
in suspension

*

in the camps
trucks load white sheets and coffins

trucks load young militants

loaded with hunger and false identity cards
loaded with stench and sacrifice
loaded with anguish
trucks start their engines

trucks race to the borders
cross over and
explode

TRULY THERE IS NOTHING MORE

Give me a child   you begged
  don't spurt onto my thighs
              take care of me
    i   refugee from a wasted country
keep me under your roof while the storm blows

            and i did

hungering for the nectar in your mouth
the lava spilling from your once dead volcano
i cupped your breasts in my adoring hands
   cupped time in my bed while smoothing your neck
 beyond words i fed off the touch
    the rightness of our enveloping clasp
        i your master   your slave
how you used me to keep self together

but now you have withdrawn   departed
and my love is denied
              deprived
                      disdained
by you who used your body to
save your body

              *

marooned on the island of your absence
i read books about the spirit-lover
death a mere breath away
   illness   theft   ridicule   mere moments away

surely the loss of your lips   your limbs
                    your perfume
          can be made up by another?

but i sleep fitfully
          will myself to flay desire
          will myself to feel no longing

and i dream of a strong man
          he holds a wolf in his arms
          the wolf's jaws are free
          but the wolf does not bite him
i dream of a strong man
          he regards the world with
          the smile of one
          who listens only for the music
          of drifting stars
          the hum of buds ripening
          the incantation of mountain streams
i dream of a strong man
          he holds a pebble in the palm of his hand
          and a dice
          he throws them both into the air
          watches as they turn and turn and
                    turn
yes i dream of a strong man
        for whom the dice land and roll
          so he laughs and cries
          then catches a pebble
          presses it into his palm
          till it bleeds

then in my dream   i dream you are
painting your features

painting in a look of calm
a look of reflection
painting your hands and throat
your toned thighs and curved hips
your ribbony lips and mounded breasts

and you paint the strong man
in the colours of earth and sky   the colours of water
you paint that strong man beside the woman you are
you paint him and her with a brown brush
your most sinuous strokes
till you and i stand together
                              naked
     and
          there is nothing   more
     to wish for
               but kiss

OLD MAN OF THE MOUNTAIN

Faceless
  neck a tree without eyes
  yet visionary

he has one ear
for stroking the streams
and the breeze

bouldering
arms and legs
   buttress the shaggy skull

dark slit between his thighs
a lair for leopards
      other wild cats

skin weathered mottled
palms sanded
     crusty with nails

earth no longer embodying him
he sits
exposed

humble and proud
looking out at
raw stars

GREETINGS, FIERCE SPIRIT
"Salvation means deliverance from all saviours."
'Report to Greco', Nikos Kazantzakis

Nikos   you roam unhindered
 far beyond in the deathless zone
plunging deeper than silence:
  your invocations   your imprecations
  your supplications   your lamentations
     your praises   your eulogies
  your enthusiasms your despairs

I have traced your steps   your sighs
across rooftops and dunes
   the adolescent alleys of Iraklion
   the resinous pines of your beloved Crete
then across the sparkling Minoan waves
   the parched jehoval sands of Sinai
   the cloying courtyards of monkish lairs
till you reached the hermit bridges of the Seine
filed past the sweat-stained tomb of Lenin

I overheard you curse manhood's desire
  how you struggled to embrace the Christ
  till you bowed to the Buddha
  watched his elephant eyes take in everything at once
I overheard you moan with pleasure
  caressing Itka's revolutionary breasts
  night after night in Berlin

how you wanted everything . . .

to become the cosmos of light and dark

and I smiled the inner smile
when you described the wise one
walking through the village at dusk
flute haunting day's end
   tiger melody to restore strength
   imbue the night with sweetness

ah   Nikos

   gargantuan lust for the pain
dripping from widows' hearts
 the humiliation of proud men cringing
before the Turkish occupier
     the flagellation of their broken spirits
     the rancid smell of stale oil

you challenged life to draw your bow
      draw it beyond breaking point
you challenged yourself to draw out the beast
      set down the crucifix
hammer out from the chaos of gas and heat
the timeless finite destiny of the human

so you lived as the bowels receive and sift
    meat and fish   grains   fruit
all they digest   extracting rejecting
then propel the eater back onto the battlefield
  so you lived traveling like Odysseus
  toothless but dogged   hero of the Hellenes
    pilgrim whose deeds you laboured over
       in your final years
slow burning beacon for your failing eyes

   Nikos

some months now I have traversed your report
   savoured each page   each chapter talking
   with the rosemary breath of fresh bread
and found you a true brother

our spirits never rest   are never quenched
from vessel to vessel life passes
O brave and bloody one
though we have sores
 we cleanse them as best we can

    a kiss for your indomitable will

TOP QUALITY

Love that blinds
  that spellbinds
that sings
   that is famous

  that love
        that sort of love
      announces itself without warning
and if that sort of love seems to ebb and disappear
    it is because such love is not that sort
         of love

that sort of love only dies if you kill it
and will not depart
           unless you force it
   so   don't be lazy with this love
don't be too casual
  and don't allow it to blind you

      don't!

  then this love will shine
     will surely and steadily shine
      thru clouds of turgid days:

       your passing whims
      your rage
      and lonely fumbling

  your sensing senselessness

DEATH AND REALITY
For Sigmund Freud

He cannot move
He sits in his house and cobwebs grow thick
The grass grows thick
His lips stiffen with disuse
His hands lie fixed at his sides
He cannot move in the hole
So deep he cannot see over the rim

He cannot even see the rim

He cannot even touch the rim

He cannot imagine anything but the rim

         *

NOTHING cannot exist   but he imagines there is nothing
worth anything

That is why he is waiting to die

         *

Now
       waiting
 is a long and tedious process

are things actually bad enough for him to actually plan
                to actually kill himself?

            it is still a joke
                a joke
    a joke between him and his girlfriend

    He has a girlfriend

                        *

    His girlfriend is also very sick   in more ways than one
                    get my drift!
    his girlfriend is also sick of living because they are not living
    with enough will to live

    the tank is on empty
    for all sorts of reasons

                            off

                        co
                        urs   e

                    *

    Of course there are reasons

    no one wants to die for no reason
    its just   reasons may vary
            though the variances are usually quite slight
        (breasts heaving with the milk of loving madness
                        cocks ready to spurt)
            conditions
            humans are born with or born into

the consequences of madness are usually painful
     madness is to be avoided   like the plague
don't make madness a plague
   examine yourself for madness

at your workplace look deeply into people's eyes
  go beyond the enslaver
                 the abuser
    go beyond the lackey and the lord

at work roll up your sleeves and
      don't worry about the powers on high
       war between the gods

don't worry about aids road deaths
     kickbacks   paybacks
keep your madness   grow your madness
make it strong   make it stronger than
  the madness that builds weapons and
other means for domination
     masturbation   elimination

indeed   once you are thorough and truthful
you will find life peaceful

  you will find

you will be surprised at what you will find

A GLIMPSE

In the restaurant
when i touch your arm
in farewell
  your look
melts the scars in my eyes

and your face
          suddenly young and tender
      desiring
    is open
          to all of me

your face   timeless and vulnerable again
to all disappointment can wring

and i too burn

          in that moment
    you have again become
                the woman i want

FREE RANGE

I plucked them out the cage
        five young hamsters
tossed them into a box
   five bright cheeky faces peering and mewing

I plucked them out the crowded cage
drove to a field at the edge of the houses
      there   lifted them   wriggling

'Go little ones
    forget the blue cup of fresh seeds
      the dripping water
run free in the veld
    scavenge   know the joy of the hunt
        the gnawing of empty forays
   the cold thrill of surviving great beasts
loss when they gobble a brother or sister

go little hamsters   never tell my son
I did not deliver you to the pet shop
        let him think you still safe
but one day when he too must venture out
I will reveal our secret   tell him
     and defend this choice'

and so they tumbled from my fingers
blinked in the sun
      disappeared into the undergrowth

THREE BROKEN WINDOWS

Across the road in the flats
three broken windows

       one a leaning tower

       one a hat

       one a tear

across the road   under a powdery vast sky
rain falls and wind blows
and blows and blows
             into the holes

into the tower lifting the hat   kissing away the tear

FINDING THE RIGHT THING

For Woody Allen

His wife leaves him
He has long left his wife
He does not know what to do with himself
She does not know what to do with herself

He sits alone in their house
Contemplating cosmologies of short term survival
She sits alone in a rented flat
Summoning congregations of spiritual advisers

He switches from channel to channel
She advertises for another man to support her

He phones an old girl friend
There is no reply
She phones Lifeline
The lines are busy

Days pass   weeks pass

He emails his wife
Admits he has made mistakes
She confirms that he has made mistakes
She returns to their home
He welcomes her home
They sit together at the dining room table
They eat together
They cannot speak
They go to bed

The next morning he and his wife stay in bed

SNAP DECISION

Why be angry?
why allow fools to break one's calm
    one's equilibrium
why allow them to disrupt?
        after all
what do they represent
if not
       foolishness?

  the horizon too distant
they lie and slurp refusing to work
bulging stomachs and pupils
       slapping thighs   belching
        locking their eyes on the
          billionaire's closet

so let *them* get angry
  let *them* be slack
greedy grasping

let them make fools

      of themselves

TRANSIT IN ADDIS

Ten hours to kill

in the gleaming tiled transit lounge
like a hotdog
shiny roll spiked with overhanging girders

I want to kill these dead hours

peel Time
nibble Newsweek
to find
half-naked women tortured in fast cars
government press conferences applauding sleek lies
school grounds ruled by steroid bullies

hours to kill

staring at Italian photos
antique scenes of Ethiopia

how I want to kill these dead hours
but not even the waitress who tells me
it's 8 birrs to the dollar
can keep me awake
not even her wistful smile
when I produce empty pockets
not even the ex-minister's memoir
about the Derg's prisoners
or the one exposing imperialist Aid as a racket
or the prayer rooms that give off
an odour of blasphemous pleasure

can keep my eyes open
can keep me from drooping

I want to burn these hours

trapped without birrs   without dollars
outside in the dark
fabled city of selassie
toothless lion of Judah
sleep soundly as dubai and frankfurt
beckon memory and travel

kill these dead hours!

echoing footsteps
new arrivals
rouse me
gaggle of green dresses clinging to thighs

I sway now   not from tiredness

stewardesses sweep out the tunnel
this is the land of the long distance runner
so lithe they must be
high heels clicking new world anthems
dashiki'd musicians play lips like drums
and the hall soars
as shambling bear catches my eye —
bushy bearded loping poet
from ghana encountered in chad
on his way to delhi
another talkfest
anther fixture on the international
trail

I am awake

we greet   murmur
then he's gone through the gates
flight via beijing
and I am left to marvel
booming laugh and strong teeth
west african excess
its rhythmic loquacity
but even our ganja-dancing
philosophizing interests
cannot justify
these ten hours outside addis

fabled city of shaggy lions and armed thugs
organized african disunity
running through its alleys
not dead
not quite alive
dawn lightens the overhead girders
the speculated city
a jumble of buildings
in a landscape of stretching plains
jagged mountains
twisting riverbeds

ten hours
captive in the bubble of transit
surrounded by earthscape fit to be the
high church of a sovereign continent

BREAD

Testimony of Roman Frister

When my father lay dying
I came to him
I saw the bread under his cap

I could not take the bread
While he still breathed

The next day
He was dead

I found him too late
My father was gone and so was the bread

Which did I miss more?
Can you answer me?
Which did I need more?
Can you answer me?

NAPOLEON'S SMILE
"Wild, obscure, saturnine, a sinister enigma"

They stood apart at first
but when they saw it
    they drew close

      *

tender and beautiful in exile
the ogre charmed friend and enemy
   the lean consul pudgy emperor
   country boy who made cities tremble

they say no bust nor portrait
truly bore his likeness
for those who stare cannot see
    quivering at the feet of power
    their eyeballs roll

so the monster with his creole love
she from dusky Martinique
  another island on the margins of imperial maps
enjoyed nights sweet with breezes
but could not warm the prison fastness

and denied the English promise of an English manor
betrayed by their fear of his compulsive movement
exposed to the cancerous rays of ordinariness
      he expired melancholy

Napoleon who turned Europe upside down
smelted a new crown to suit himself

exhausted France but made her great
at 45 became a legend not just a tyrant

*

the thirst for immortality   unquenchable
   they drew close   tried to draw him close
tried to draw him   tried

      till he drew to his close

*

once on a battlefield he spied
a dog wandering
      a dog once fed by a soldier
now wandering on the battlefield
a dog once sheltered beneath her dead master's cloak

a wandering dog that brought tears to the emperor
drew tears from his heart

a lonely hungry dog on the battlefield
   those killing fields of freedom

YOU LIVE IN A HIGHRISE SLUM MADE OF PORRIDGE

You live in a highrise slum made of porridge
i in the mountain fastness of philosophical truth
we come together after you have washed and ironed and swept
after i have drugged myself with theory

we come together on the bridge of our bodies
fold into each other
                `   join

*

i offer you my dialectical tongue   babble the seeds
you offer me fragrant ripe breasts

your moist lips keep me stammering
as we climb stairs because the lifts have burnt out
and the landlord can't afford to replace them

we open the door of your bedroom
   the smell of incense covers
the garbage in the alley beyond the window

then i hold you and we make love
you and i in the numberless city
  hungry and in need

we make love and the city is a hum in the afternoon
a hum that cannot drown out our cries
   you and i
     stirring the pot of our pleasure

SERIAL SHAME

We can shed lives   shed faces
  shed self
act out compulsion
   hurt to dominate

       *

serial killer from olivenhout
  twenty-two women
        tied their mouths with cloth
     left a bottle in each vagina
killer man
      such loneliness
      such blindness
      such secret smiling
      such bragging
      such bragging to himself

  stalking planning stalking
killer man scouring olivenhout
   in the bushes behind the shacks

olive tree of the crucifix

  such hate   such hate
such pleasure when they beg
      once they are dead

such loneliness

BLACK DOG

The little black dog is dying
drags his hind-legs
        lingers in the kennel
    whines at all hours
        won't eat

the little black dog is dying
    spinal column falling apart
    discs collapsing without a chance to rebuild

abused by drunks as a pup
saved from the gutter
    we gave him a yard
a patch of grass
    but he never stopped cowering

we fed him bones and gravy   mash and dry biscuits
        but he never stopped staring
fierce wounded eyes expectant of beatings
        never stopped snapping
        never stopped shying away

but today when I gave him his pill
he licked my hand   licked my face
he swallowed that pill in one gulp
        the pill that makes the pain
        that will not go away
                    go away

at last the little black dog
showed he cared

to be held by the touch
that shows care

the little black dog   dying
licks his way back to life

NIGHT THOUGHTS FROM BOYES DRIVE

The view makes me think

Parked high above the ocean
      road hugging the mountain
melancholy wind bending
everything to its will
          flattens bush
makes me feel sadder than radio cackle:

> *Be my body tonight*
> *Please baby*
> *You want my money*
> *I want your honey*

talkshow has these kids
      hi frequency: Motivation   Inspiration
  gangsters
trying to break out of pimping
  tik

> *Be my body tonight*

phone in from some woman who adopted aids orphans
  she's cool
then   melody from malmesbury
who came to town for adventure
      for bucks

she's sweet
courted by a married somebody
from mitchells plein
      he concealed his wives and kids
      impregnated her in the back of a bakkie

near macassar
took her in the arse
then called her his pussy
made her mad oiling her clit
and she rode him past dawn in a moan and a fury

months later she lost the child
when he pounded her stomach

melody's a domestic now in somerset west
3 days a week for a nurse somebody
whose old man is a doctor in worcester
but whose kids show respect
she likes kids with respect

melody who sang at the road lodge
duets with hi fliers
now burbles her oath to love jesus

*

muizenberg beach fringed by waves
like a zigzag heart machine
then crashing into kalk bay
spraying fishermen
with salt and wild water

i love the wind and the night
and i shiver
knowing   that little by little
grand buildings tarnish
maintenance goes astray
refurbishment funds go missing

even the courthouse crumbles
president's palace a playground for spiders
        no surprise when they fall into the sea

city excavated thousands of years from now
will show scum on its neck

                    *

the view from boyes drive
makes me breathe faster

    the view
                        inspires me
            gladdens me
just like melody in the morning when the bucks keep her warm
        and she forgets her rape-baby

i read the weekend papers
speculate why writers are asked about politics:
        i mean
        governments never stop lying
        bankers never stop fleecing
        journalists never stop scooping idiocy and genius

that's why
 the view from boyes drive makes me wish
for a mature woman

MATING

Beyond the ripening moment of ejaculation
   of ovulation   of ululation

apart from the mind's making of dreams
      the body   in its touch and feel
            creates mythology

   beyond orgasm

            in the moments of subsidence
            of serendipitous calm
               when breath steadies

   in those moments of acknowledgement
   that joy was reached

in those moments I love you
   most

MAPUTO
December 2007

Eels slither from the fishing harbour into dusky streets
women drag plastic buckets filled with scaly suppers
gardens name rose bushes after heroes of independence
at the Accor hotel plastered whores plead with drunken tourists
while purple neon tarts the casino skyline

I pass a newspaper stand: (ex-president)
CHISSANO WINS MILLIONS for not taking millions
while millions disappeared from the central bank
and the journalist Carlos Cardosa was murdered
to keep the thieves safe

I pass Standard Bank's glittering palace
South African capital making hay while the sun sets
on Stalinist folly
further north the coastline snapped up
for human development:
            golf estates   holiday flats
                    shopping centres
all owned by the pale and swarthy preachers
of trickle-down theory

in the avocado-strewn courtyard of the National Library
the marble statue of a Portuguese cardinal-emperor
pisses on the wall's pile of broken bottles
in a restaurant near the beach and the embassies
three peroxided mulattas giggle over beers
trade unionists cut fish steaks sauced
with international solidarity

I watch the waves
palm trees bending in the breeze
slender mobile supple trees
standing tall after civil war and seasonal floods
after macheted arms can no longer hold or give love
after the Rhodesians and the Boers have gone and returned
and now a foreign aid economy stutters
between bread riots

CROSS

She loved him for his way with words
his sparring
      placed a white flower in her hair
      sat at his feet
      fetched rare wine
      from deep in her cellar

he was warm to her
that winter
generous but wary
shared his thoughts
  hands that maddened her need

she wore dresses
clutched her thighs
lay down and whispered
of long journeys without a staff
and he drank her broth
caressed but did not kiss her

so it was:
      she offered herself
      he offered friendship

she never forgave him

RED ANTS

The red ants come in the morning
they find the people asleep in their beds
the red ants hammer on the doors

the people refuse to open their doors
the red ants bore through
and enter the living rooms

the people protest
demand to know on whose authority
they come with their pincers

the red ants hold up an order
a court order
their order

the people examine the letterhead
pour over its contents
whisper in corners

the red ants grow restless
the order now stained with children's tears
grandmothers' snot

the red ants shout:
clear out
we must do our work

the people run to their bedrooms
lock the doors
peer through the keyholes

the red ants fume
acid builds up their heads
they grow redder

the people huddle in bathrooms
barricade toilets
block fire escapes

the red ants dissolve the doors
pile beds and fridges
onto the landings

the red ants swarm over their toys their pots
till their linen their books their tv's their socks
jam up the landings

the people are befuddled
try to comfort their kids
try to comfort themselves

then the people cry out:
don't you dare throw us into the street!
don't you dare dump us in the cold!

but the red ants clear the building
snort the dust in the corners
scour webs from the cupboards

and while they work the red ants sing:
pay your rent! pay your lights!
pay everything and we will disappear into the walls

pay everything and we will leave you
poor ones drunk ones lazy ones
leave you to yourselves

and the people
the ones who want to pay but cannot
the ones who can pay but do not

the poor people of the slums
watch the red ants swagger
bits and pieces between their mandibles

too late to talk
too late to organize:
everything's smashed

SONG FOR MY CHILDREN

You leave the dock   *(clap hands twice quickly)*
        powered by the clock   *(clap hands twice slowly)*
Moon peeps out of hiding   *(clap hands once)*
        waves are rising   *(clap hands three times slowly)*
Your ship's now sailing   *(clap hands three times quickly)*
        though deck has no railing   *(clap hands twice)*

I have launched you   *(clap hands once)*
        I have rocked you   *(clap hands four times)*
The sun will light you   *(clap hands once)*
        sun will burn you   *(clap hands five times quickly)*
Salt make tasty   *(clap hands three times quickly)*
        salt make crusty   *(clap hands twice slowly)*

Sweet birds of spring   *(clap hands once)*
        may cause the heart to sing   *(clap hands seven times quickly)*
Will you be serious?   *(clap hands six times slowly)*
        be spared the grievous?   *(clap hands eight times quickly)*
One thing is certain   *(clap hands once)*
        times you'll be hurtin'   *(clap hands once)*

But your ship must sail   *(clap hands five times slowly)*
        though wild winds wail   *(clap hands ten times quickly)*
Be calm on deck   *(clap hands three times slowly)*
        fear no wreck   *(clap hands three times slowly)*
Learn to sail 'free style'   *(clap hands three times)*
        this voyage lasts for just for a while . . .   *(clap and clap   and
clap. . . at first slowly then faster and faster and faster . . .)*

RIVERBED

Mud   pools
flecks of birds and flies
  tracks of wind and dogs
long distant rain will come too late
for rotting leaves and branches
dragged down
  giving off the stench of death
  and the life to come

in the riverbed two boys hopalong
one with short steps
    the other stretches far into the future
        bold boy that
                        bold

behind them   man with a staff
    man
still game for battle
        though bowed by ecstasy's demands
        her bleary mornings
bowed by the clink of coins
wishing well of the have-nots
    the diseased
bowed by drought and flood

the boys run
  prize a crab out of the mud
run on the grey slate
        crushed and sharpened when glaciers
        collapsed and compressed
they skip over a bird

rotting for ants
cracks for the bones
   burnt mud splitting into diamonds

*

after the snow in the mountain melts
and the river runs
      the boys will fish again
      the man will throw down his staff

warrior-man and young boys
      cutting the surface as they swim
   grey slate of the riverbed
   liquifying mirror for their strokes

BATTY

Old farmhouse   walls high as a cliff
forest of beams support the mottled ceiling
            the infinite stars
and there in a crevice   kink in the wood
lives a bat
                a tiny inky bat   soft as a heart

as sunset bloods windows
the old man   who lives in the house
leaves fruit on the table
and the grey mouse who lives under the table
sprinkles pieces of cheese

then when electric light shows up the shadows
the little bat flies from table to floorboard
spreading her heart-shaped wings
darting   this
            way
                        and
                    that
till there is no more fruit on the table
no more cheese in the cracks

        she sweeps clean
for the old man and the mouse
and I   stranger come to prove
blood is thicker than water
    that ghosts have names
I catch the little bat
                        tiny inky bat
    hold her close in the night

and in the morning when she squeaks to be free
I let her fly to her beam in the ceiling
watch the old man fill the bowl
    the mouse cheese the boards

all three of them   in the farmhouse
  and I the famished stranger

FOR G.

On the road   from the road
drug haze of the summit
hotel
used by those addicted to use

escape from yourself
break yr neck to break the face that stares
back and drags you back

once by a river you played me
your long pipe
        your hollow root
a plaintive enigmatic music
and when I walked away to return home
you stayed cross legged
by the river
       etching the vibration of the universe

you forgave us all
you always forgave
everyone
        but yourself
peaceless spirit
hung from a branch in a place of the dead
now gone
yet remembered

peaceless sweet spirit

PRAISING SHEMBE

Nathi lives in Raleigh Street near Kenmere
works in a panel beater's shop
    father works at a chemist nearby

over Xmas went back to the Berg
stayed with a family of sangomas
but didn't like what was going on with muti
  he had come to find SHEMBE
    SHEMBE in those mountains
   in those valleys   in those clouds
  in those thunder storms   SHEMBE high up

Nathi did not wait to be dirtied
     petty ambition and stupids
     selling muti for money and sex
he's on the way back to Jozi

      now listen to Nathi   aka Norman
he's available   for any job in the city
   any job that will keep SHEMBE alive
in his heart
       he is ready to help and make things
       good for you

  so give Norman a call
when you need him
  when you need a job done
     any job

here's his number   his father's number
  please say 'i will be sure to give him a call'

SHIFTING

Moonlight

shadows   of   branches
                    how they dance
splinter
       a white curtain

dark branches gracing the white
       charcoal come to play
spilling across the milky window
behind them

                    *

tree and window
       ghost life under lamplight

windy night
                    dream shadow dance

       shows itself
branch on white

branches of moon brighten
       the curtain dance

dancing yellowy light
       before   between   and past   midnight

Mi luv i long 4 u

mi monee 4 rent isnt enuf
baby pleez ph zodwa 2 lend me 200

> *have spoken to zodwa*
> *she will lend you 200*

thanx sweetee
i wil lend u mi hart

> *she made me promise to pay her back*
> *if you cant*

thanx darling

> *when r u going to get a job*

don't b + lovee
did mi asking friten u

> *no*

don't b fritend hunee
u wil get mor luv from mee
than u ever hav

> *I hope so*

i long 4 u mi sweethart
if onlee i kood tuch u now

> *when are you going 2 get*
> *a job*

r u angree with mee mi luv

> *no*

u sound so +

> *no*

i want 2 make u hot an happee

> *i should hope so*
> *actually I want the same for you*

thanx mi sweet
its good 2 no u wish mee 2 b happee

> *what else do you want from me*

2 b mi won an onlee

> *you are*

an u 2

> *glad to know that*

sleep wel mi darling

> *sleep tight and look for a job*
> *in the morning*

PAPGELD
Maintenance Court

They come to force
old partners
      dead-eyed men in slack jackets and well ironed jeans
        worn socks and pouching cheeks
            exes
    sometimes lobola paid but no further due delivered

they come to force these men:
      maintain your coughing kids in nappies
    in woolen caps   pap and panado

  these mothers
alleged to be shrews   cold or barren
   abandoned for firmer breasts and redder lips
    plumper or sleeker thighs

they come to enforce
   jam on the table   bones in the pot
with sleepless eyes
   2 o'clock rockings and four o clock hushings
they come to force the fathers to father

bristling before the ways of the law/lord
   they come to court favour
from the magistrates
   toothless black robes deafened by the wailing
   or spruce professionals with sharp tongued hearts

these mothers plead:

support   us   zealous angels of stale desire
hours   so many chewed striding corridors
  slouching on coffin shiny benches
hour after   hour
heavy   our lives

though freed of desertion   of drunken fists
  freed of sullen silence
names called   and not-called
  noses rubbed   hair pulled
by the chill of icy fuming clashes
hour after   hour   pleading for their errant men
  to be thrown inside or straightened out:

          'after all   he is the father of my children
    why would I want him to sit in jail?
    why would I want to poison him?
          why would I make him go barefoot?
          go down the drain?'

demanding these men be brought to book
            by the Good Book
        the book of numbers
              the law of contract
        the book of the law of the land
        damn!   bring the bastards to book!

the mothers sit and shake their heads
    milk pouring from ample breasts
  while white walls blank evidence
            renounce their testimonies
        drown out their oaths

the mothers swear before the court:

he who has opened his fly
must make a plan
must come right
must cough up!

these large and slender women
still fat with after-birth
demand the law take its course
take up their cause

they come
in the name of
the sacred children of sour kisses
these women
stretching the tension in the brittle chain
of
life

NORTH BEACH, ART STAMPEDE

Fording the Umgeni   ignoring
the hotels   the joggers   the geriatrics
amaZulu herds come down to the beach
and reach the promenade
        one with wings   one with sunglasses
         one with a violin strapped to her back
        one with a rubber assegaai sticking out the side

paddling at low tide   parading technicolour udders
papermache horns pointing skywards
  styrofoam tails flicking sand flies
        all the colours
prancing along their fabricated flanks
        these bovine beasts make artistic feasts
        for passersby who care to examine the spectaculaire

and lolling in the shade
herdboys with sharpened sticks
make sand sculptures
    curvy dolphins   pointy breasted bikini bathers
      sea serpents and baby crunching crocodiles
herdboys with fluorescent teeth
as they milk for coins

   hola!
succulent amaZulu herds at the beach
rainbow teats and haunches
ready to hoist horns while they raise the dust
       of art's rejoicing

THE WAR PARTY AND THE DEFENDING PARTY
Depiction of a San rock painting on the wall of a guesthouse in the Cedarberg

The gathering warriors   male and female
ascend a slope towards the cave
                its overhang

the defending party clusters
    releases a volley of arrows and spears

                below
the attackers halt   run two lines of power
    merging beyond the battlefield
    the power lines run to the feet of an astral traveler

    this long striding man-creature
ahead of them
        looks back at the war
                    and leaving it behind
                travels forward

            only the new star remains
            and half a moon

            *

We heap a fire with dry wood

figures dart in and out of the flames
  in and out of sight

    how vain we are!
imagining our names count in time

how vain to think of names

how quiet the night
          only mosquitoes disrupt defecation
    only meditation will take out their sting

the war is surely over
  power lines connected
 the traveler surely on his way

above us the vast myriad pulsing sunfield

MAD PAINTER

Mad painter came to this canyon
   tattered brush
  can of black paint
and when the hawk called
above the roar of the river
  he splashed the black paint
  along the rock face
  let it drip
    down
  the yellow stone
  trying
to make
   his mark

PREDATORS

u inspire desire and loss
   gay and bitter laughs
        sharp anger

 i was slave to you
junkie
   do anything u pleased

 but in yr casual stupidity
 u took too much
   kissed me into a casualty

now despite yr calls
i summon strength
  to deny u

and when i resist
 u first sulk   then beseech
both   leave me shaken

the answer remains
       we won't meet again
   prey   to each other

WHALES IN FALSE BAY

"What hurts the soul?
To live without tasting the water of its own essence"
                                    Rumi

The first day
I sat at a wicker table
in a house tucked under the hill
tracked the whales heaving
     humping across the bay
massive flanks and fins
breaking the surface
exciting me
                stirring me
   spumes beading the air
commotion rising from great depths

grey whales
scaled shells clinging to their vast bulk
cousins I say
we are related
               ancient cousins
you make me want to gush
and part the waters

O great foaming sea   wash and guard them!

                    *

the second day
I scoured the surface waiting for magic
to break

                    for blubber to
shoulder white horses

I sat at the wicker table
confirming wind-born ghosts still stay
fresh as the south easter
        melancholy and desire lingering with heat
        justice hungering for downtrodden bergies

clouds rolled over the mountain
        edgy rim of the table where good gods
        and the devil smoke

childhood city
            now I'm an orphan
time mists my glasses
I burn with images
caress myself   stroke savagely
    when no love can be gleaned

Cape Town
            tucked away
safe
except for marauding
gangs stalking drink and drugged flatlands of
sadness and shame
    harsh as alcohol fumes
lifting the skirts of a Khoi Venus
            loose light filling features
            with the legacy of loitering

the wind that carries fish and salt
to mix with the mustiness of
unwashed whores

*

the third day
I sat at the wicker table
dreaming of sleep
and the words of Rumi

     mantle of jokester wisdom
   to wash away cares
     'after giving the heart
       wallow in friendship's warmth'

so I spun a queen into being
made her love me for my balls
loaded her with jewelry and other shininess
till brandy couldn't keep her drunk
     my declarations so sincere
  stroked her everywhere till she came with me
to a higher place
   and smiled   and danced with me
  danced over me and
          sighed

that queen played my instrument
at the free concert in the park
  a fantastical lover who brought forth
  fit sons and daughters
but a mob accused her of witchcraft
 of holding me ransom
 of burning me with a fire unbecoming age

     fire that ought long to have been extinguished
child's fire babbling in the dark
    raving mantras supplicating

Fate
to live beyond the revs
deemed safe

yes I was bewitched!
              what muti did she sprinkle in my tea?
hosting phantoms from dervish tales
who consume   convulse
    lead from discretion

and I called out:
          please Universe!

grant me the cups of her breasts
the silky lather of her fountain
allow me the insanity
of her joy
          let no jinn destroy
the bleat of my serenading
  make limp my rod
now keeping time to that holy music

*

the fourth day
          a bubble waiting to burst
I was relaxed
      relieved of burdens

scattered over the bay
cousins dipped and dashed waves
          I became ridiculous
tripping on these beauties

foaming with emotion as the ocean
washed wishes into a froth

again I conjured my Muse
          black 'n blonde barbie
          dimpled cheeks missing a tooth
she lit my eyes   threw off her sandals
          as I declared:

creature of my fever
allow me to seed your womb with majesty
while in the bay whales propel steadily
          ancient blood churning the depths
            of planetary life

                      *

on the fifth day
I bit my pen   called the hosts of fellow learners
     disciples pupils   to order:
            no more carousing   no more buying and
selling in the marketplace
   no more fornicating with scratchy cats

I called them to the tasks
set by our master

I conducted a class
            bowed my head
   cleaned the nib and the stick
          steadied my hand as I whipped up
spray and seagull shit

there at the wicker table

facing the bay
          salt streaming from my eyes
     while whales spooned with their young
I spoke Rumi out of my heart
          wrote him into the marrow of my soul

WHO KILLED STEVE BIKO

A Boer
A group of Boers
The Boers

Who killed Steve Biko

Shallow minds
Vanities of power
Outrage provoking outrage

Who killed Steve Biko

Superior weapons
Alien diseases
Internal discord

Who killed Steve Biko

Kickbacks
Bacterial hospitals
Arm steals

Who killed Steve Biko

The black diamonds
The white cynics
The frayed rainbow

their sentiments, their prejudices, their passions; and they would not stand unmoved if their kinsman or countrymen were shot down after their rights have been continuously and contemptuously trampled under foot. Is the doctrine that blood is thicker than water for ever to be applied to one section of the population only? At a crisis like the present every man, worthy of the name, must take up a definite stand, however he may regret the necessity which forces him to it. To hesitate is to play into the hands of those who are trying to wrest from us our birthright, and deprive us of our heritage. We call upon all Cape-Colonists to declare themselves on the side of progress, pure politics and fair play—it is the winning side, the odds for ignorance, corruption, and oppression are already nowhere.

With the country Boers, living in almost entire ignorance of the end-of-the-century developments, and wrought upon by social incendiaries, we can sympathise, however much we may oppose. But what shall we say of those among us who are seeking to suck no small advantage out of the life-blood of their own hard-pressed countryman? What shall we say of the South African Telegraph, or, rather, of those who are manipulating the columns of our contemporary for their own personal and party ends, who are poisoning the air with the foulest insinuations—the excrescences of unscrupulous opportunism? The real traitors are those who are yelping "treason" at Johannesburg and Jameson, who take advantage of the crisis to attempt to stab their political opponents in the back, and who would sacrifice honour, principle, consistency, nay, the lives of their fellow-countrymen, for the paltry purpose of a party advantage. Faugh! The plot is too transparent, too utterly contemptible, to require further comment. The great moral to be drawn from the situation so far is the wonderful success which a show of force has had upon President Kruger. The uitlanders have for years agitated constitutionally in vain, now, with an armed demonstration, they are promised much. It is deplorable that the President and his Hollander underlings should show themselves only amenable to such arguments, but, of course, the uitlanders took him somewhat unawares, before he had imported all his Maxims, his seven-pounders, his skilled Continental mercenaries, or built his frowning forts —all out of the uitlanders' earnings. The uitlander must literally to prepare the lash wherewith he was to be tortured. Now if he is to gain his concessions he must take care to have them down in black and white or not at all. As for Dr. Jameson we can at this hour only wait, but we are profoundly thankful that in the main, the Cape Town judgment of Jameson has been fair, generous and free from party spirit.

For Painless Extractions, gold and other fillings, artificial teeth of highest quality, and an exact imitation of natural teeth, set in other gold, platinum, celluloid, or vulcanite, and at about one-third the ordinary cost, go to the London Dental Institute, Water Chambers, Greenmarket-square.

Mourning Outfits—Special line. Black Worsted Suits to measure, &c. M. Lyon's Time-Clothing Stores, Plein-street. [1684

influence, a new and ordinary era would be instituted, and with a remodelled Executive all the abuses and corruption would be speedily swept away and instead of a sullen opposition to the reasonable wishes of the people they would be freely taken into the confidence and asked to aid the efforts of one who has always had their interests at heart.

I would look back to the time when the Chief Justice took his present position at the early age of twenty-seven, and on his arrival in Pretoria the annexation had taken place, it is a well-known fact how he became a persona ingrate with Colonel Lanyon through his love of justice and opposition to the arbitrary proceedings of that officer, how he has been the means of giving confidence by his fearless actions in defence of the integrity of the High Court.

The present crisis would, I know, never have taken place had not a deaf ear been turned to the earnest advice rendered by him to make reasonable and just concessions, and to meet the just demands of the people; but now I fear that an obstinate clinging to power will prevent the President acting in a way to restore confidence, as this would do.

The wonderful and rapid progress of the country is getting beyond Paul Kruger, and the sooner he retires in favour of a man who, like the Chief Justice, is so well-tried, and has the confidence of all, the better we shall then have peace, and the power of all sinister and hurtful influences will be broken, and a purer and more just system of Government prevail.—I am, etc.,

AN OLD BURGHER.

TO-DAY'S POLICE COURT.

(Before Mr. G. B. WILLIAMS, A.R.M.)

ALLEGED THEFT.

Sandhill, a Kafir, was charged with having stolen a leather satchel, valued at 9s. 6d., containing £2 15s. and some papers, the property of another Kafir, a harness-maker, of 87, Aspeling-street.

It was alleged that the prisoner took the satchel out of the prosecutor's box, and that he then locked the box and took the satchel to his room in Roeland-street, where it was found.

A remand was granted.

SHOP DOOR THEFT.

A Kafir, named Boer, was charged with having stolen a jacket from the shop door of Mr. H. W. Markham, Adderley-street.

Prisoner was seen to coolly take a jacket off a nail, and walk away. He was convicted last month of having stolen a pair of trousers, and there were other convictions against him. He was now given three months' hard labour.

MISSING WINE.

John Milton Town and Edwin Schwartz were charged with having stolen an eight gallon cask of pontac, valued at £2, belonging to Messrs. Sedgwick & Co. Prisoners were employed by Messrs. Sedgwick & Co., and it was alleged that on the 21st of last month they had a cask of wine to deliver, which they failed to do. The cask in question was afterwards found on the possession of the prisoners.

Mr. A. Brittain appeared for the defence, and a remand was granted until Saturday.

WATCH SNATCHING.

Christian Fokker, a coloured youth, was charged with having stolen a watch by snatching it from the person.

Last week a complainant was assaulted at the public station by two natives. It was said that a gold watch had been snatched from his person. He gave his number as 4,072, and a detective subsequently made. Detective search of this man prisoner yesterday, when he found on the prisoner a gold watch, but had lost it. The complainant said that the man who had snatched the watch was not the prisoner. He alleged that he did not see the man that snatched it. He would not give evidence.

A remand was granted.

IN AND OUT OF THE OCEAN

The captain scuds over the waves
ocean glitters with his spit
sun shrivels as he turns

the speedboat forces its way
the centerfold woman dangling over the rails
offers him everything

headless fish become food for the gulls
night falls
the speedboat runs out of fuel

radio crackles with sos's
the centerfold woman goes below and takes off her veil
the gulls tire of hake

the captain rams her
gulls squawk
the boat drifts

the captain snores
the centerfold woman folds into two
while he dreams of her sister

                    *

the male mole fish is one tenth the size
of the female and attaches himself
to the female with special teeth

after a few weeks he becomes permanently fixed
gets food through her bloodstream
supplies her with a permanent stream of sperm

the male mole fish and the female mole fish
have a very settled relationship

MOUNT ZION

Exhibit of a Torah-Shirt

A building of yellowy white and green
    sandstone and thyme

King David's tomb smudged with books
open on the laps of Ethiopian boys
        embroidered skullcaps fastening curls
        their teacher sways before the silver scroll-holders
        the cloth drums and trumpets
        accompanying David's harp

strings caressed tenderly for the virgins
        the mothers with full breasts
        the mothers who cry for their warrior sons and husbands
        whose blood spills in the valleys and along the coastal dunes
        and in the alleyways of Ashkelon

King David singing of the ten thousand cities
destroyed by the Swastika
           pits piled high with corpses

the air of Europe forever
ashen

             *

a building of white and green
nurtures racks and glass boxes
exhibits of debris
The Thousand Year Reich's trail

bloodied and gutted

exhibit A: shirt made of Torah scroll

instructed by a Nazi under pain of death
the Jew-tailor selects passages that curse
   five thousand year diatribes
   cross the desert
    dry wind blowing from the wadis
   to choke the throats of Amalek

and the Nazi who parades
at Gestapo headquarters
the Nazi in his Jew-shirt strutting
   at a fancy dress party in Stuttgart
    on the Fuhrer's birthday
  then a celebration in an Alpine lodge
    wife serving the Fatherland with another son
   and a friend's wedding to a pure
     Aryan sow

Nazi does not know
Jew-tailor dresses him in abject surrender

the Temple falls   again and   again
but it will rise though death-trains run on time:
   ARBEIT MACHT FREI tattooed
   on the parchment of starved arms
   Jew-sacrifice brought to the blood-gods
   to fertilize the Reich

*

King David rides the trains
harp wailing
hair torn   tunic soiled with faeces

David rides the trains
sings to the Nazis
and the Nazis proudly wear their Torah shirts
        as they pull the levers
        as they pull the pins
        as they pump in gas and release their dogs

King David sings
        and the psalms
      robe the Jews in sad pitiful hope
           of an after-life

Heroes of the Hour: 18h00, April 26
Found poem as composed by Business Report

1

Siemens chief will step down in the wake of a bribery scandal
in times like these the company needs clarity
about its leadership
kleinfeld was the 11th chief executive in the company's
160-year history

siemens informed investors about the allegations
after police searched company buildings and the homes of
employees at 30 german locations

siemens appointed kleinfeld chief executive after
he helped turn around us operations
by cutting back unprofitable divisions
and removing 10,000 jobs

under kleinfeld
siemens underwent some of the most sweeping
transformations in its history
when he inherited the company net income per employee
was less than one fifth of general electric
more than half the main divisions lagged
behind profit targets

siemens sought to reverse sliding earnings
partly by making employees work longer hours for
no additional pay

2

pepsico fizzes past forecasts
as first quarter profits rise 16% to $1,1billion
or 65c a share
on the strength of its international
beverage and fritolays snacks divisions

3

seldom punished 'liar loans'
will prolong United States housing slump

new century financial
the second largest us subprime mortgage lender
filed for bankruptcy on april 27, 2007

ameriquest mortgage charged borrowers extra fees
and it is a common and open practice
for account executives to forge or alter borrower information
or loan documents

according to the financial crimes enforcement unit
mortgage fraud complaints more than doubled in the us
from 2000 to 2006
and suspicious activity reports increased fourteen fold

4

shares in j sainsbury surged 7%
after an unidentified buyer snapped up a 14% stake
in the uk's third largest grocery chain

the swoop ignited speculation

that a new takeover bid
was being prepared two weeks after the company
rebuffed a bid by private equity groups

5

colgate palmolive's profit in the first quarter gained
50% on sales in latin america
as demand for swivel headed toothbrushes
and other products kept rising
and helped gain market share from rivals
proctor & gamble

sales increased 12% to $3,21 billion
the company's shares have jumped 19 percent last year
for their top annual gain since 1999

colgate had 37 % of the us toothpaste market

in december 2004
colgate embarked on a 4 year restructuring progam
that called for eliminating 4,400 jobs - 12% of the workforce
and closing a third of its factories

6

royal bank of scotland
santander central hispano and fortis
have offered $72,2 billion to buy ABN Amro
sparking the biggest ever takeover battle
in the financial services industry

the royal bank led group offered $39 a share
with 7% in cash and 30% in stock

its approach was 13% higher
than the all-stock bid abn amro accepted
from barclays two days ago

7

the first assets from fidentia holdings
the cape–based financial services company
at the centre of south africa's biggest white collar swindle
are to come under the hammer this month

the curators have instructed auction alliance
to sell off office equipment and cars belonging to the company
as well as gym equipment originally destined
for the boland rugby union sponsored by fidentia

it is believed that between R900 million and R1 billion
have not been accounted for
much of the money is alleged to be due to
widows and orphans of miners

8

welcome to the michael milken institute global conference
at the los angeles beverly hilton
a fire marshall's nightmare crammed with people
who have money or power,
want money and power
or are willing to pay several thousand dollars
to be near any and all of the above

at least 3000 people are packed into this high powered salon
where they can hobnob with the junk bond king turned philanthropist
and tycoons like murdoch, pickens, turner and broad

when the conference debuted in 1998
the world was still reeling from the asian market meltdown
and organizers struggled to fill seats
milken the 1980's wall street wizard whose creative financing
landed him a two year sentence on securities fraud
was till fresh out of prison

but today the event has grown into a confab of Hollywood heavyweights
political and academic stars
and even the occasional olympian
and milken and his family have funneled more than $1 billion
into medical research and education

9

women make up 46% of the uk's 376,000 millionaires
and the numbers are growing by almost 11percent a year
on the back of social changes such as inheritance trends
the rapidly climbing divorce rate and a new generation
of women who are entrepreneurs

while a male millionaire's wealth grew 9,2%
on average over the past eight years
the worth of a female millionaire ballooned by 53,9%

*

no doubt
about it

things are getting better . . .

PERHAPS

There at the station of arrival
            station of olives bread and wine
  your familiar tangle of hair

        and in that moment
                    i am relieved
for your face and your body
correspond to the source and the memory
of words

      identifiable and mysterious
you are stories of advance and retreat
there in the headlight of my need for intimacy
    writhe snakes I cannot lift
            onto the altar of your thighs

you are a moaning
            a mouth turning towards then away
you are a hand at the table
    you are a partner in a life

    will it be this life?

HOW MUCH STRONGER

Passing from loneliness
   to
solitariness

      from despair
         at defeat
   to equanimity

this is the way it must
        turn out
  this is the way . . .

your tears in the meeting
for the dead and maimed of the war
astound the committee

some comfort you
but all think you are broken
without reason

       stricken messiah
little do they know you are
so much stronger than them

BABY SEVEN BILLION
31 October 2011

You are lying there
Not naked
Already swaddled in cloth

You are lying there in a stainless sterilized
Cocoon

You are lying there at the raw edge of a city
Where water and jobs are scarce

You are lying there in the arms of a mother
Who is a Madonna

You are lying there untouched
Because your mother has died

You are lying there with all your limbs
Corresponding to the right number

You are lying there shriveled
By a genetic malfunction

Baby

Baby seven billion

Two of you every second
Have we passed a point of no return?
Tokyo's thirty-seven million
Lagos's fifteen

What does my I amount to in this multitude?
But till
Tomorrow
I have all the time to live
Till tomorrow

And now I will be your father
Baby seven billion
I will stand by you
I will do my utmost
With all my weakness
All my madness
I will do my utmost

to bring you a tomorrow

SKY WALKER

More than ever
The love lack bites

More than the ganja
More than the hum of machines
More than the tastes and smells
Of the mind orgasm
Brought by the penis

More than all this
The utter moment
When in philosophizing
An exquisite art
Is celebrated

Sky walker

SEED TO CESSATION

Everything in   passage
everything   shaped by and shaping the passage
everything   in anticipation   apprehension
          of the passage

now be confident
          wait for the future
receive from the pasts all their presents

make a present of the present
          everything in passage

everything comes to pass
once its present